Death Valley Desert

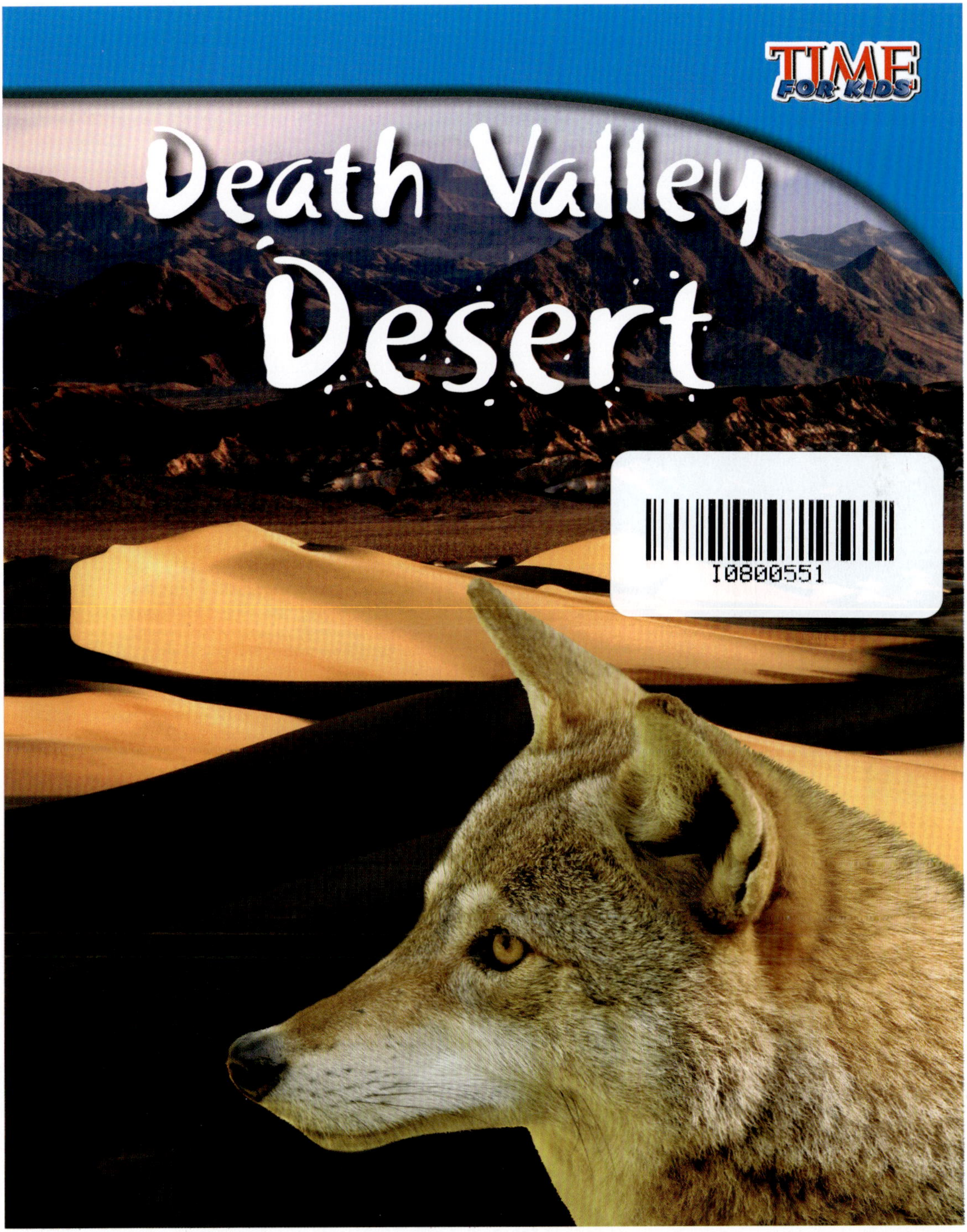

William B. Rice

Consultant

Timothy Rasinski, Ph.D.
Kent State University

Dixie B. Lass
Registered Geologist

Publishing Credits

Dona Herweck Rice, *Editor-in-Chief*
Robin Erickson, *Production Director*
Lee Aucoin, *Creative Director*
Conni Medina, M.A.Ed., *Editorial Director*
Jamey Acosta, *Editor*
Heidi Kellenberger, *Editor*
Lexa Hoang, *Designer*
Stephanie Reid, *Photo Editor*
Rachelle Cracchiolo, M.S.Ed., *Publisher*

Image Credits

Cover Doug Lemke/Shutterstock; inset: Kenrick Griffith/Shutterstock; p.2-3 kavram/Shutterstock; p.3 Brzostowska/Shutterstock; p.4-5 Mike Norton/Shutterstock; p.4 Qweszxcj/Dreamstime; p.5 kavram/Shutterstock; p.6 left top to bottom Cheryl A. Meyer/Shutterstock; Robyn Mackenzie/Shutterstock; Sarah Scott/Shutterstock; p.6 right top to bottom: Mark Yarchoan/Shutterstock; Lee319/Shutterstock; p.7 top to bottom Jeffrey T. Kreulen/Shutterstock; Sarah Scott/Shutterstock; p.7 inset: Eky Studio/Shutterstock; p.6-7 kavram/Shutterstock; p.8-9 KAZMAT/Shutterstock; p.8 Dorn1530/Shutterstock; p.10-11 Sasha Buzko/Shutterstock; p.10 Monika Hunáčková/Shutterstock; p.11 ndrpggr/Shutterstock; p.12-13 KenCanning/iStockphoto; p.12 top to bottom: skydie/Shutterstock; Sebastien Burel/Shutterstock; Bill Perry/Shutterstock; p.13 top to bottom: JohnSeiler/iStockphoto; EuToch/iStockphoto; p.14-15 N Mrtgh/Shutterstock; p.14 SGC/iStockphoto; p.15 top to bottom: NNehring/iStockphoto; Rodney Mehring/Shutterstock; p.16-17 Steve Minkler/Shutterstock; p.16 JonTimmer/iStockphoto; p.17 Photomyeye/Dreamstime; p.18-19 Sai Yeung Chan/Shutterstock; p.18 Darren J. Bradley/Shutterstock; p.19 bottom: Wikipedia; p.20-21 kavram/Shutterstock; p.20 top to bottom: Arnoud Quanjer/Shutterstock; p.20 Lasenby/Shutterstock; p.21 top to bottom: Paul Chesley/Getty Images; Jerry Young/Getty Images; p.22-23 kavram/Shutterstock; p.22 middle: Martha Marks/Shutterstock; p.23 top to bottom: J. S. Fisher/Shutterstock; Nelson Sirlin/Shutterstock; p.24-25 Galyna Andrushko/Shutterstock; p.24 left to right: LOC-USZ62-101280; LOC-DIG-npcc-19914; p.24 inset: Michele Bagdon/Shutterstock; p.25 top to bottom: LOC-LC-USZC4-2483; Richard Peterson/Shutterstock; akiyoko/Shutterstock; p.26-27 Gordon Wiltsie/NGS Image Collection; p.26 top to bottom: Rue des Archives/PVDE/; Mariusz S. Jurgielewicz/Shutterstock; p.27 kavram/Shutterstock; p.28-29 Pichugin Dmitry/Shutterstock; p.28 top to bottom: PHB.cz (Richard Semik)/Shutterstock; Bob Keefer/Shutterstock; p.29 top to bottom: fotokik_dot_com/Shutterstock; urosr/Shutterstock; p.30-31 Bill Perry/Shutterstock; p.32 Galyna Andrushko/Shutterstock; back cover: Lee319/Shutterstock

Based on writing from *TIME For Kids.*

Teacher Created Materials
5301 Oceanus Drive
Huntington Beach, CA 92649-1030
http://www.tcmpub.com

ISBN 978-1-4333-3672-0

Printed by: 590835
Printed in: China

Table of Contents

Got Water? 4

Geography and Climate 8

Plants 12

Animals 16

People of Death Valley 24

Glossary 30

Index 31

About the Author 32

Got Water?

There is a **desert** in California called Death Valley. There you will find places called Badwater Basin, Coffin Canyon, Deadman Pass, Funeral Mountains, and Starvation Canyon.

Does this sound like a good place to visit?

BADWATER BASIN
282 FEET / 855 METERS
BELOW SEA LEVEL

Actually, Death Valley is a beautiful place to visit. It is full of life and interesting landscapes. It is especially famous for the wildflowers that bloom there in the springtime.

But how in the world did the places in Death Valley get their names? Death Valley has **conditions** that make it difficult to live there. It is extremely hot and dry. If you ever visit there, be sure to bring plenty of water!

desert paintbrush

Death Valley Blooms

Wildflowers in Death Valley are a beautiful sight—if you know when to find them. The chart below shows the best times to look for wildflowers.

wildflowers

Geography and Climate

Death Valley is in eastern California. It is a very deep valley surrounded by tall mountains. It is the lowest place in the United States. In fact, it is lower than sea level—about 282 feet lower!

Death Valley is part of the southwestern desert area of the United States. Deserts do not get much rain. Death Valley gets less than two inches of rain each year. That's not much.

Little rain means that the ground stays very dry most of the time.

NEVADA
Death Valley National Park
CALIFORNIA
SIERRA NEVADA
CALIFORNIA
Death Valley
Pacific Ocean
N
E
S
W

Most deserts are hot places. Death Valley is a very hot desert. During the summer, it can get to more than 105°F during the day. It's also hot at night. Summer nights are about 85°F.

How Hot Is It?

The highest temperature ever recorded in Death Valley was 134°F. This is almost twice as hot as the average temperature in Los Angeles, California.

The ground in Death Valley is quite salty. This happens because of **evaporation**. When the air is hot, any water on or near the top of the ground evaporates. Salts that were dissolved in the water are left behind. In some parts of Death Valley, you can find salt all over the ground. The main area where this occurs is the **salt pan**.

In the salt pan, you can actually see salt on the ground, as these close-up photos show.

Plants

All living things need water to be healthy. As you know, Death Valley is a dry place without much water. So, do plants live in Death Valley? You might be surprised to learn they do. However, the plants are small and grow far apart from each other.

Be Prepared!

The high temperatures, lack of water, and dangerous animals make the desert a potentially dangerous place. It's also easy to get lost in the desert, so make sure you always stay in a group. When traveling in the desert, it is important to be prepared. Make sure you always:

- Bring lots of water.
- Wear clothing that protects your skin from the sun.
- Wear protective shoes.
- Avoid actions that cause you to sweat.
- Stay away from snakes, spiders, and other insects.
- Watch out for cactuses.

Tough Plants

Desert plants survive harsh conditions. They have to **adapt** to the environment.

The creosote bush is one of the most common plants found in Death Valley.

Plant Protection

Plant Protection
Needles protect the plant from thirsty animals.
Thick waxy leaves and stems store water.
Deep long roots search for water underground.

One plant that lives in Death Valley is desert holly. It grows in the hottest and driest parts of the desert. It can go for many weeks, or even months, without water.

Like most people, most plants do not like water or soil that is salty. The desert holly is one of the few plants that likes salty water and soil. But, there are places in Death Valley, like the salt pan, where it is too salty for even the desert holly to live. In these areas, no plants grow.

cactus rose

A cactus will often have a flower bloom like this one. Even in the harsh desert, plants can be beautiful.

Pickleweed also lives in Death Valley. It grows in the areas with a lot of water in the ground. Pickleweed needs more water than the desert holly needs. It also likes cooler weather than the desert holly does. But, in the places where pickleweed grows, it is still hot.

Strangely, pickleweed likes salty water and soil, too! Of all the plants found in Death Valley, pickleweed can handle the most salt. In fact, pickleweed lives on the edge of the salt pan.

Animals

Animals need water to live, too. There are many kinds of animals that live in Death Valley. They all drink from small pools of water in the desert.

Bighorn sheep are often seen in Death Valley.

Watch Out!

Tarantulas are large, hairy spiders that can live up to 40 years. They are common in Death Valley. They catch and eat other insects by running after or jumping on them. For moisture, they get some of what they need from their prey!

tarantula

One large animal living in Death Valley is the coyote. Coyotes are like wild dogs. They howl at night and wander all over Death Valley. They go into the valleys and up the mountains. They even go across the salt pan. Other animals do not go there.

coyote

The kit foxes in Death Valley are very curious and friendly. Sometimes they visit people who are camping and beg for food.

kit foxes

Kangaroo Rats

The kangaroo rat is another animal that lives in deserts. Kangaroo rats are a lot like mice. They have long back legs and hop like kangaroos.

kangaroo rat

Scorpions are like spiders. They have eight legs, but two legs are actually claws. They use their claws to catch insects and eat them. Scorpions also have long tails with stingers. They sting bugs and animals, including people!

Glow Bugs

Scorpions glow if you shine them with a special light called an **ultraviolet light**.

Horned Lizards

The horned lizard is an unusual animal that is common in Death Valley. It has horns on the back of its head, on its chin, and on the sides and back of its body.

The sidewinder is a snake. It lives in desert areas like Death Valley. The sidewinder does not crawl on the ground like other snakes. It forms its body into an *S* shape and crawls across the ground sideways. Only two or three parts of its body touch the ground at a time. It does this because the ground in the desert is usually hot. This keeps the snake's belly from getting too hot. It is also easier to move across the desert sands this way.

sidewinder rattlesnake

Believe it or not, there are fish that live in Death Valley. They are called pupfish. Pupfish only grow to about three inches. They live in **marshes** and small pools made by springs of water. These marshes and pools are very salty, like the ocean. The pupfish has adapted to live in these salty shallow waters.

pupfish

Turkey Vultures

Turkey vultures are common in Death Valley. They are very large birds. Adult turkey vultures have a **wingspan** of six feet. There are no feathers on their heads.

Many kinds of birds live in Death Valley. One is the roadrunner. Adult roadrunners are about two feet long from head to tail. Like most birds, roadrunners can fly. But they prefer to walk and run on the ground. They run very fast. Roadrunners are fast enough to catch rattlesnakes. They are quick enough to catch hummingbirds and dragonflies in the air!

Quails

Quails are common in Death Valley. You can spot them by the feathers that stick straight up from their heads. Baby quails follow behind their mothers in a line. It looks as if they are playing follow the leader!

quail

a roadrunner eating a lizard

People of Death Valley

American Indians came to Death Valley many years ago. But, they did not live there year-round. Sometimes they camped and hunted in Death Valley, but the tribes often moved from place to place. Sometimes they did not go to Death Valley for many years.

Today you might find arrowheads, spearheads, and bits of pottery they left behind.

The next people to come to Death Valley were looking for gold. They came in 1849 during the California gold rush. They did not plan well for their journey. It was very hot and dry. Many of the people died in Death Valley. That is how it got its name.

American Indians are the first people known to have lived in the Death Valley area.

Americans from the east came to Death Valley with the hope of becoming rich by mining for gold.

Colored Bottles

Bottles made of clear glass were left on the ground in Death Valley by **miners.** Over the years, ultraviolet rays from the sun turned the glass bottles purple.

More people came to Death Valley in 1881 to mine **borax**. Borax is a **chemical** used in various cleaning products. People picked up or dug borax pieces from the ground. Borax was packed and then **hauled** to the city of Mojave. Many mules were needed to move the borax.

Mules played an important part in mining operations.

Metal containers like this one were used to transport borax.

Scotty's Castle is one of the most famous places in Death Valley. It is a ranch house built in the 1920s by Albert Johnson. It was named for Walter Scott, Johnson's friend. People called him Death Valley Scotty.

Scotty's Castle

Death Valley is famous for its beauty. It was made a **national monument** in 1933 so it can stay beautiful and natural.

Almost 1 million people visit Death Valley each year to see the landscape and camp near the wildlife. Perhaps next year, one of those visitors can be you!

National Park

National parks protect areas of land for future generations.

This flower will turn into a piece of fruit. Humans can eat the fruit after careful preparation.

Glossary

adapt—to change to fit a new or specific use, situation, or environment

borax—a mineral that is used mainly for cleaning

chemical—a substance with its own unique composition of molecules

conditions—states of being; circumstances

desert—dry land with few plants and little rainfall

evaporation—the change by which any substance is converted from a liquid state to vapor

hauled—pulled or dragged

marshes—areas of land that usually have wet, soft ground and grassy plants

miners—people who dig into the earth in search of gold or other valuable resources

national monument—a place of historic, scenic, or scientific interest set aside for preservation, usually by the president

salt pan—a big area of flat land that has a high amount of salt on the surface of the ground because of evaporation

sea level—the height of the surface of the sea midway between the average high and low tides

ultraviolet light—a special type of light that people cannot see

wingspan—the distance between the tips of a pair of wings

Index

American Indians, 24
Americans, 25
arrowheads, 24
Badwater Basin, 4–5
bighorn sheep, 16
borax, 26
California, 4, 8–9, 24
California, Los Angeles, 10
Coffin Canyon, 4
conditions, 6, 13
coyote, 18
Deadman Pass, 4
Death Valley National Park, 28
Death Valley Scotty, 27
desert, 4, 8, 10, 12, 14, 16, 21
desert holly, 14–15
dissolved, 11
evaporation, 11
Funeral Mountains, 4
gold rush, 24
horned lizards, 20
Johnson, Albert, 27
kangaroo rat, 19
kit fox, 19
marsh, 22
moisture, 17
Mojave, 26
national monument, 28
pickleweed, 15
plants, 12–15
pottery, 24
pupfish, 22
quail, 23
rain, 8
roadrunner, 23
salt pan, 11, 14–15, 18
scorpion, 20
Scott, Walter, 27
Scotty's Castle, 27
sea level, 8
sidewinder rattlesnake, 21
spearheads, 24
Starvation Canyon, 4
tarantula, 17
temperature, 10, 12
ultraviolet light, 20
United States, 8
vultures, 22
wildflowers, 6–7
wingspan, 22

About the Author

William Rice grew up in Pomona, California and graduated from Idaho State University with a degree in geology. He works at a California state agency that strives to protect the quality of surface and ground water resources. Protecting and preserving the environment is important to him. He is married with two children and lives in Southern California.